PEOPLE IN ART

Clare Gogerty

Artwork: Annabel Spenceley

CHERRYTREE BOOKS

A Cherrytree Book

Designed and produced by Touchstone Publishing Ltd
68 Florence Road, Brighton, East Sussex BN1 6DJ, England

First published in 1994 by Cherrytree Press Ltd
a subsidiary of The Chivers Company Ltd, Windsor Bridge Road
Bath, Avon BA2 3AX, England

Copyright © Cherrytree Press Ltd 1994

Designer: David Armitage
Cover designer: Tim Peters

Cover picture: *Self-portrait with Bandaged Ear*, Vincent Van Gogh

British Library Cataloguing in Publication Data
Gogerty, Clare
    People in Art. – (In Art Series)
    I. Title II. Series
    707

    ISBN 0-7451-5210-4

Printed and bound in Italy by STIGE

Contents

In every chapter of this book you will find a number of coloured panels. Each one has a symbol at the top to tell you what type of panel it is.

Activity panel Ideas for projects that will give you an insight into the techniques of the artists in this book. Try your hand at painting, sculpting and crafts.

Information panel Detailed explanations of particular aspects of the text, or in-depth information on an artist or work of art.

Look and See panel Suggestions for some close observation, using this book, the library, art galleries, and the art and architecture in your area.

 Portrait of the artist

Mirror image

When you looked in the mirror this morning, what sort of person did you see? Were you smiling, or grumpy, or sleepy? Or was your face quite still? Do you think your reflection gives away what kind of person you are?

Ever since mirrors were invented 500 years ago, artists have been looking into them and painting what they see. These pictures are called self-portraits. Many artists choose to paint themselves because it's easier and cheaper than hiring models to pose.

Choose self-portraits from this chapter or elsewhere and think what the artists might have been like in real life. Make some notes describing each artist's personality. Then find out about the artists and see if your descriptions are correct.

◀ The boy in this picture is posing for his portrait. But there is no artist to paint him; he is taking his own photograph. He has attached a piece of string to the shutter of a camera and is about to pull it. Look at his expression and what he is wearing. What sort of impression do you think he is trying to create? [Self-portrait, Norman Rockwell]

Character clues

A self-portrait usually tells you what the artist looks like physically. But, more than that, it provides an insight into his or her personality. Even if an artist has a straight face in the portrait (they usually do because it is difficult to hold a smile or other expression for very long), there are other clues to look for. Are there frown lines on the forehead, or smile lines round the eyes? What about the artist's posture? Is it slumped with exhaustion, relaxed, or stiff and proud? What about the possessions or surroundings in the picture? Do they tell you what the artist was interested in?

Your many faces

You look different depending on how you are feeling and what you are doing.

What you need
• sketchpad   • pencil   • mirror

What you do

1 Sit in front of a mirror and pull some faces. Smile, laugh, look angry, unhappy or puzzled.
2 Choose two or three expressions and try to hold them long enough to draw them. See how your face changes with each expression.

(If you find it too difficult to keep an expression and draw it at the same time, ask a friend to take some photographs of you making different faces. When the film is developed, copy what you see.)

The artist in society

The popular idea of an artist is a poor, struggling, lonely genius. But artists are not always poor. Many have been, and still are, successful and wealthy. Artists sometimes use self-portraits to show other people their achievements and their status in society.

Albrecht Dürer, who lived in Germany 400 years ago, was a popular and respected artist. He painted his first self-portraits when he was only 13, and went on to paint many more. Fascinated by the shape of the human body and by facial expressions, he thought the best way to learn how to portray them accurately was to practise on himself. He liked to paint himself in the height of fashion and obviously enjoyed wearing and painting fine clothes.

▲ *By portraying himself in fine clothes, the painter of this self-portrait wanted to show that he was a gentleman and not (as many people in the fifteenth century believed artists to be) simply a craftsman.*
[Self-portrait with Gloves, *Albrecht Dürer*]

Rembrandt's dressing-up box

In the Netherlands during the seventeenth century, many of Rembrandt's fellow country-men wore sombre, black clothes and white ruffs. But Rembrandt lived near the port of Amsterdam and often saw traders from foreign countries, such as India and Turkey. Their clothes were much more exotic. Excited by the rich colours and the fine fabrics of which they were made, Rembrandt bought outfits from the traders and kept a collection of them at home.

As well as dressing in these clothes and painting himself, he also painted other people wearing them. He loved the way light fell on silks, satins, velvets and other rich fabrics and transformed them. He was also fascinated by the way jewellery sparkles in the light.

The heart of the artist

▼ *Compare the two self-portraits below. They are both of the same man, Rembrandt. The one on the left was painted when he was young; the one on the right when he was old. How do you think he was feeling when he painted each one? Look for clues in the expression on his face and the clothes he is wearing.* [Self-portrait as a Young Man *and* Self-portrait in Old Age, *Rembrandt*]

Anyone looking at a portrait forms an opinion of the person they see. Aware of this, artists sometimes bend the truth to make themselves look richer, or more attractive, than they really are.

The Dutch artist, Rembrandt lived a hundred years after Dürer. He painted about sixty self-portraits, from his youth to his old age. Although he was a popular and fashionable artist as a young man, he fell out of favour in his later years and lost all his money. Despite the change in his circumstances, Rembrandt still wanted to impress people and went on painting portraits of himself dressed in extravagant clothes and looking confident and prosperous.

Although the fine clothes in his later self-portraits might fool you for a moment, the expression on his ageing face gives away his real feelings – of sadness, failure and despair. In each of his self-portraits you can see behind his features right into his heart and mind.

Portrait pairs

The way you see yourself is probably quite different from the way other people see you, because they see you when you are unaware of yourself – in different moods and engaged in all kinds of activities. Find a friend to help you with this experiment.

What you need
- pencil or piece of charcoal each
- paper or sketchpad
- mirror

What you do

1 Sit in front of a mirror together and draw your own reflections. Draw quite quickly and loosely. Start with the general shape of your heads and then fill in the details.

2 Then sit face to face and draw each other.

3 Compare your self-portraits with the portraits done by the other person. Do they look similar? If not, how are they different? Why are they different? Is it because of the way each person draws, or the way each person sees the other?

Torment in colour

Vincent Van Gogh, another Dutchman, also painted many self-portraits and, like Rembrandt, was not afraid of exposing his feelings in his pictures. Van Gogh was a man of strong emotions.

Unlike Rembrandt, however, Van Gogh was never rich or fashionable. Although he is famous now and his paintings sell for millions of pounds, he was poor and unhappy all his life and suffered from bouts of mental illness. Eventually he committed suicide.

Van Gogh believed that colour was the most important thing in a painting and that it had the power to change the way people felt. He thought that a dark-blue sky brought on feelings of dread, for example, whereas yellow made people feel happy and cheerful. Van Gogh's paintings are full of bright, vibrant colours in unusual combinations. You might not think of using green or yellow when painting a face, but Van Gogh did, and to great effect.

In his self-portraits, the combination of strange colour and thick brushstrokes that dart across the paper give the impression of an unhappy, troubled man.

▲ When Van Gogh painted this self-portrait, he was feeling very depressed. He was recovering from a breakdown during which he had cut off the lobe of his ear. Look at how he has painted his face with many small brushstrokes, creating a feverish impression. Only his eyes are still.
[Self-portrait with Bandaged Ear, *Vincent Van Gogh*]

# 2 Painting other people

A portrait is a likeness of someone, so any photographs you have of your friends and family count as portraits.

Leonardo in Italy

There have always been people, called patrons, willing to pay artists to paint. During the fourteenth and fifteenth centuries in Italy, many rich and influential people, such as the important Medici family, commissioned artists to paint their portraits.

Leonardo da Vinci began his career under the patronage of Lorenzo de' Medici. Leonardo introduced a new style of portrait painting. He painted realistic pictures that showed the personality of the sitter. Before this time, faces looked flat and not very lifelike. Very few were based on real people.

Leonardo used colour in a delicate, sensitive way and did not use any hard outlines. Each tone of each colour gradually merged into the next, creating a soft, hazy effect that Leonardo called *sfumato* (meaning 'smoked').

▲ *This is probably the most famous picture ever painted. It is a portrait of a woman called Mona Lisa. The artist has captured the personality of the sitter by using thin layers of paint. This creates a delicate, mysterious atmosphere. Mona Lisa's expression has puzzled people for centuries. Why is she smiling? Does she have a secret?*
[Mona Lisa, *Leonardo da Vinci*]

10

▼ *King Henry VIII of England commissioned Hans Holbein to paint this portrait of him. Henry, dressed in his fine costume and jewels, and with his solemn expression, looks commanding and ruthless. Centuries later, the picture gives us a sense of what he was like.*
[Henry VIII, *Hans Holbein*]

Leonardo was an important influence on other Italian artists of this period, such as Raphael and Titian. Raphael studied Leonardo's paintings and used many of his techniques in his own portraits. Titian painted many wealthy people in fine clothes. These portraits are full of rich colour, creamy highlights and sketchy brushstrokes.

Inside an artist's studio

When you paint a picture you may have to use the kitchen table or draw in a sketchpad on your lap. Professional artists usually work in studios with big windows to let in as much light as possible.

Artists mostly work standing up with the picture in front of them on an easel. Oil paintings are painted on canvas, a thick cloth made from cotton. The canvas is stretched across a wooden frame and then nailed to the back. This makes a tight, flat surface to paint on.

If you had your portrait painted, you would either go to the artist's studio or the artist would come to you. You would be called the 'sitter'. People paid by artists to sit for them are called models. Some artists have favourite models that they paint many times. It is hard work posing for a portrait – you have to stay in the same position for a long time, and perhaps return several times for more sittings.

In fifteenth-century Italy, when Leonardo was painting, and in the eighteenth century when portrait painting was especially popular, successful artists had assistants working in their studios. The assistants would paint the large areas of the picture, such as the background and the clothes, and the 'master' would fill in the face, hands and other important details.

Painters go to court

Royal families have always been great patrons. Even today, monarchs commission artists to paint their portraits.

In the sixteenth century, King Henry VIII paid a German artist, Hans Holbein, to work for him. Holbein's main job was to paint portraits of Henry and his family but he also painted other important people. His pictures are very detailed and include every hair and wrinkle. Holbein often placed his figures in surroundings that explained their position in the world – a merchant with documents around him, for instance.

Leonardo and Titian from Italy, Reynolds from England and Velázquez from Spain also travelled to the courts of Europe to work. Their task was to glorify the monarchy by producing flattering portraits of the royal family.

Portraits of the grand and famous have been popular in all cultures. Ancient Persian books, for example, contain portraits of nobles, and in the Nigerian kingdom of Benin, in Africa, sculptors carved idealized images of members of their royal family.

Fame and fashion

It is not easy to paint a flattering portrait that is also an honest likeness.

On the walls of any stately home, you will see grand and dignified portraits of the owners' ancestors. In real life they may have been less attractive and imposing, but of course they wanted to look their best. Anthony Van Dyck, a court painter in England 200 years ago, was

◀ *Three hundred years ago, in what is now part of Nigeria, Africa, there was a kingdom called Benin. Its kings lived in palaces decorated with sculptures, including brass heads like this one. Although it is of a real person, it is not a true likeness but an idealized version.*

▼ *The two people in this picture were wealthy English landowners. They were painted outdoors on their estate. All the land you can see was owned by them, and they commissioned the portrait to show other people how important they were. Look at their expressions. What do you think these people were like?*
[Mr and Mrs Andrews, *Thomas Gainsborough*]

Paint a portrait

Paint a portrait of someone you know well – a member of your family or a close friend. Include the whole body in the picture.

What you need
- sitter
- room with good light where you can leave your materials out after each session
- easel if you can get one, or a board to rest your paper on
- large piece of paper
- pastels or paints

What you do
1 Think what your sitter should wear and how he or she should sit in order to be comfortable and feel at home.
2 To stop your sitter getting bored, choose a time when an interesting radio or television programme is on.
3 Sketch your sitter's overall shape before filling in the details. Use colour to reflect a mood – bright colours for a jolly portrait, cooler greys and blues for a thoughtful pose.
4 Props will help put across the personality of your sitter. A young sister might want a teddy on her knee or a sports-mad friend might look good in sports kit.

popular because his portraits were always flattering.

Although artists usually painted kings and queens sitting stiffly side by side, they would paint other people at home, more informally, as if the couple or family were passing a quiet Sunday afternoon at leisure.

These informal pictures of two or more people were known as 'conversation pieces'. (Not that the sitters were talking to each other: it was considered undignified to show people with open mouths.) Thomas Gainsborough was an artist who painted conversation pieces. The surroundings are an important part of his pictures, showing the wealth and good taste of his patrons.

Modern and free
Today, artists like to paint portraits of their family and friends or pay models to sit for them. This gives them the freedom to paint what and how they like. They do not have to worry about painting a flattering portrait to please a patron.

Just as we all have different handwriting, so each artist has an individual style.

Look at as many portraits as you can – old and modern, from your own country and other cultures. Note how the artist has painted the facial features. Are they detailed and realistic, with reflections in the eyes and lines on the lips, or sketchy and impressionistic? Try to see why an artist has used a particular technique and what effect this has on the feeling of the portrait.

Grant Wood, a modern American artist, painted a realistic but disturbing portrait of a couple (see above), quite unlike Gainsborough's conversation pieces. Wood's style was realistic and detailed. His paintings look 'finished' and have no sketchy areas or loose brushstrokes. Van Gogh, on the other hand, used wild brushstrokes and unlikely colours. Amedeo Modigliani, a twentieth-century Italian artist, distorted the shape of the face and body of his sitters so that they look sad and appealing. All these artists captured the likeness and character of their sitters but the techniques they used were quite different.

The changing face

People's faces change as they get older, but you can always see a similarity between a young face and an older one. You will need an adult's help with this project.

What you need
- photograph of your older person when he or she was young
- pastels
- sketchbook

What you do

1 Study the photograph you will use to sketch a portrait of the person when young.
2 Pay careful attention to the details. How big are the nose, mouth and other features? Look at the position of the ears in relation to the eyes. Keep everything in proportion.

3 Now sketch the person in real life, looking carefully at the same details. How has the face changed? What about lines and wrinkles? Do they show someone who has laughed a lot, worried or been sad?

3 Figures in the round

Artists use all kinds of techniques to make figures look real in their paintings, but no one is really fooled. Painted figures have only two dimensions – width and height. Sculptures have an extra dimension – depth.

You can walk around a sculpture and look at it from

◄ The ancient Greeks worshipped many different gods. This is Apollo, the god of light, poetry, music and healing. Gods were considered to be perfect beings, so sculptures of them had no physical imperfections. This statue is made of bronze; many others were carved from marble and then painted in different colours.

▶ *This wooden figure comes from Africa and shows a warrior about to go into battle. It is not a very realistic model of a man: the legs are too short and the body is stiff and lifeless. Nevertheless, it is still recognizable as a human being. Look at the patterns on the face and body. They were made by heating a metal tool and using it to burn marks into the wood.*

all sides. You can touch it and feel its solid shape. A piece of sculpture occupies space like a real person.

Although the shape of the human body has not changed much over the centuries, the way it has been represented in sculpture has.

God-like figures

Ancient Greek statues had the bodies of ideal human beings. Because they often represented gods, they had to be beautiful, solemn and dignified. There must have been plenty of short, fat or skinny people in ancient Greece, but sculptors were not interested in reproducing realistic people; they wanted to bring the gods down from the heavens to walk on earth.

Greek sculptors studied skeletons and learnt how bones affect the shape of the figure. They saw how muscles change shape when the body moves, and copied the way clothes fall around the figure, creating a sense of movement.

Exotic sculpture

Early Indian sculptures, carved to adorn temples, also depicted gods and goddesses. The figures of Siva, Vishnu and Krishna are lively and energetic and, like Greek sculptures, perfectly formed.

Primitive carvings from Africa often served a religious purpose too. These figures, carved out of a single piece of wood, were used on special occasions such as at initiation and healing ceremonies. Unlike the Greek and Indian figures, they are simplified versions of the human body and are often out of proportion, with stylized features. They are, nevertheless, beautifully carved and full of life. Look for primitive carvings from Africa, Polynesia and Indonesia in museums.

The great Italians

In fourteenth-century Italy, scientists began to learn more about the human body and how it works. These new discoveries were useful for artists and sculptors, too.

Leonardo da Vinci studied human anatomy and made many sketches of different parts of the body. He was so keen to create realistic figures that he cut up more than thirty dead bodies to discover how they worked.

Michelangelo was especially interested in what happens to the muscles and bones when the body twists and turns. Before he started to carve a block of marble,

▲ *Although this sculpture is of four people, it is carved from one piece of marble. The artist has skilfully arranged the figures into a single, tight group. The sculpture shows the scene from the New Testament of the Bible when the dead body of Jesus was taken down from the cross. There is a great feeling of sadness and heaviness in the sculpture. How do you think it was created?* [Pietà, *Michelangelo Buonarroti*]

Look out for statues in parks or outside public buildings. Who do they represent? Why are they there? They are likely to be national or local heroes, soldiers or important politicians. A good example is the huge statue of Abraham Lincoln (right), former president of the USA, which sits on top of Capitol Hill and looks down protectively over Washington DC.

Find out as much as you can about the people represented in the statues you see.

Sculptor at work

Sculptors use all kinds of materials. Different types of stone, including marble, granite, limestone, sandstone and alabaster have always been popular. Some sculptors use bronze, others wood or even plastics and waste material such as tin cans and old bicycles.

Stonecarvers work directly from a block of stone. But for bronze sculptures, the artist first makes a model, then a mould of the model and then a cast in bronze. The whole process takes time and is hard work.

Sculpting in stone
This is how you would carve a figure in stone.
1 Use a mallet (a hammer with a large head) and a punch (a pointed tool) to knock out the basic shape from the stone.
2 Use a square hammer to define the shape, and chisels to smooth over any rough bits.
3 Polish the stone with rasps, files and abrasives.

Bronze sculptures
This is how to sculpt a bronze figure.
1 Build a framework of the sculpture in wood and metal.
2 Wrap clay or plaster around the frame and model it into the right shape. (Bake clay models in a kiln until they are hard.)
3 Now apply a layer of wax to the model and fix wax rods at angles all over it.
4 Apply a layer of plaster all over the model and leave the wax rods sticking out.
5 Put the whole sculpture into a kiln to harden. The wax will melt away, leaving a cavity between the frame and the plaster shell.
6 Pour molten bronze into the cavity and leave it to cool.
7 When it is quite cool, chip off the plaster and reveal your work of art.

Michelangelo imagined that his figures were trapped inside. By chipping away at the stone he felt he could release them. His marble figures look like real people who have been painted white.

Sculpture today
Auguste Rodin, a modern French sculptor, shared many of Michelangelo's ideas. He, too, liked the idea of freeing his figures from a block of marble. Many artists today still like to create life-like sculptures. Others have different ideas.

The English sculptor Henry Moore looked first at the shape of the stone he was about to carve, not the shape of the person. His figures are not at all realistic, but are still

◀ *Many of the sculptures by Henry Moore are based on forms found in nature. This figure is recognizably human, but it also reminds us of stones worn smooth by the sea, or a twisted branch of a tree. See if you can find any natural things that look like people.*
[Recumbent Figure, Henry Moore]

obviously human and convey powerful emotions.

Alberto Giacometti, a Swiss sculptor, is famous for his bronze statues of tall, thin figures with large feet. You won't see people like his on the street, but their stretched, skinny forms show strong feelings of loneliness and fear.

Life drawing

Some of the most famous paintings and sculptures in the world are of the human figure. Sculpting a full-size figure is a specialized process and needs expensive tools and materials. Instead, why not ask a friend to model for a life drawing?

What you need
- friend in a swimsuit
- easel or artist's board
- pastels or watercolours

What you do
1 Ask your friend to pose for you.
2 Sketch quickly before drawing in the details.
3 Try to apply your understanding of bone structure and muscle shape to your drawing.
4 Pay attention to the shadows falling on the body, giving it shape.

Looking at people

Although all human beings have the same body parts, their hands, eyes, feet and noses are all different. One person may have large, square hands with stubby fingers, another long-fingered delicate hands. Your mother may have round, laughing eyes, your sister almond-shaped eyes that are dark and menacing. Noses vary, too, and are important in giving personality to a face. Practise a little and you will improve your powers of observation as well as your drawing technique.

What you need
- accurate picture of a skeleton
- pictures of muscle structure in a biology book
- sketchbook
- pencil or pen and ink

What you do
1 Look at the skeleton. See how some bones are long and wide, others small and delicate.
2 Look at the muscles and think how their shape affects the shape of the body.

3 Draw different parts of your own body, then find volunteers to model their hands, eyes, noses – any parts of their bodies you find interesting.

4 Family in the frame

Do you have a group photograph showing all your family together at a wedding or other special celebration, or perhaps on holiday?

Painting family groups is harder than photographing them. It is difficult to get a good likeness of an elderly grandparent, a teenager and a baby, think up an interesting composition, get everyone to sit still *and* show a connection or special feeling that links all the family members.

Status symbols

In the past, many families liked to have paintings of themselves to hang on the walls of their homes. They provided a sentimental record for future generations and – because portraits were very expensive to have painted – they showed that the family was wealthy. Like grand houses and fast cars today, family portraits were regarded as status symbols.

In the Netherlands in the

▲ *It is amazing to think that this picture was painted more than 300 years ago. The clothes are different from those of today but the people look very familiar. There is such liveliness and activity among the group that it looks freshly painted. Notice how the artist has linked each figure to another so that no one is left on his or her own.* [Family Group in a Landscape, *Frans Hals*]

Shadows on the wall

A family portrait took a long time to paint and was expensive so, in the eighteenth century, many families chose a quicker, cheaper method of keeping a record of themselves. They commissioned an artist to paint their silhouettes.

The artist would use a candle to cast a shadow of the model's profile on to a piece of paper on the wall. He then drew round the edge of the shadow, cut it out and painted it black.

Most people found life-size silhouettes too big. So the artist copied the original in a smaller size, glued it on to a white background, and framed it so that it could be hung on the wall.

seventeenth century, wealthy families would hang paintings of themselves in the front rooms of their houses where passers-by could see them through the windows.

One of the most popular Dutch portrait painters at this time was Frans Hals. His style was relaxed and informal and he liked to show family members in lively conversation. His paintings are like snapshots – they show one moment of family life, frozen for ever.

Silhouettes

Silhouettes or shadow pictures are simple and fun to make. A group of them gives you an opportunity to compare noses and other physical features in your family.

What you need
- family members to model for you
- helper
- chair for model
- bright lamp
- piece of chalk
- large piece of black paper

What you do
1 Ask one of your models to sit on the chair, sideways to the wall.
2 Shine a bright light on to your model's face so that the shadow of his or her profile is on the wall.
3 Ask a helper to hold a piece of black paper behind the shadow, or pin it up if it will not damage the wall.
4 With your model sitting quite still, chalk carefully around the shadow on the black paper.
5 Now take the paper down and cut out the profile, just inside the chalk line so it does not show.
6 Glue the silhouette on to a piece of white paper. Add further silhouettes of other members of your family in a straight line or in another pattern.
7 Put your silhouette portrait in a glass-and-clip frame and hang it on the wall. Can your friends guess who is who?

Look at the clothes worn by Hals's family group (page 22). The fashions of a particular time and place can tell you a good deal about the life people led. When people wear stiff, formal clothes it often means that their lives are formal and strict, too. In more relaxed times, people wear casual or perhaps elaborately decorated clothes. Look at what people are wearing in each picture in this book and think what kind of lives they might have led.

◄ *At first glance, the figures in this painting look like an ordinary family. In fact, they are the Holy Family – Joseph, Mary and the baby Jesus. We can tell this because of various clues that the artist has included in the picture: Joseph is shown with carpentry tools and Mary is wearing a blue dress, which is how she was traditionally portrayed. Do you know which story from the life of Jesus this picture is telling?*
[The Holy Family, William Strang]

English formality

English aristocrats also commissioned pictures of their families. Most of these paintings are much more formal than those by Hals. Families wore their best clothes and sat or stood in stiff, uncomfortable positions. Like the Dutch paintings, they were meant to impress people with the family's wealth and social status.

The Holy Family

The Holy Family (Jesus, Mary and Joseph) has inspired many artists. The story of the journey to Bethlehem, the birth of Jesus in a stable, Joseph working as a carpenter, and the young Jesus preaching to his elders in the temple make interesting paintings that appeal to everyone, not just to people who believe the Christian story.

Madonna-and-child pictures show Mary and Jesus without Joseph. Early examples are of Mary seated formally on a throne with Jesus on her knee. Because

▼ *This painting of a mother and child is in a modern style but its composition is similar to that of much older madonna-and-child pictures.*
[Mother Bathing her Child, *Mary Cassatt*]

people prayed in front of these pictures they expected to see solemn, holy images. Raphael and Leonardo da Vinci, painting in fifteenth-century Italy, made the Holy Family look more like real people with human feelings. Later artists, such as Georges de La Tour, made them look even more ordinary, so that people could identify with them. This trend continued

Composition

Have you ever seen a painting by the modern American artist, Jackson Pollock? He enjoyed splashing paint on to canvases in seemingly haphazard patterns. Most artists, however, plan their paintings carefully. The planning of a painting is called its composition.

To compose a picture the artist first has to decide what is its focal point, or centre of attention. This can be anywhere, but is often in the centre. Other objects in the picture draw the eye towards it.

Sometimes the focal point is at the top (apex) of a triangle. The head of the most important figure might be at the apex of the triangle, with less important figures at the bottom angles of the triangle, leading the eye to the focal point.

into the nineteenth century. Although few artists today use the Holy Family as a subject for their work, modern paintings of mothers and their babies are often influenced by madonna-and-child pictures.

Group painting

It takes skill to make a balanced, attractive composition with more than two figures. If everyone stands in a row the picture looks flat and boring. Instead, the figures can look at or touch each other, be grouped around the tallest or most important figure, or be seen sharing an activity like a meal. Artists use these devices when painting family portraits.

▲ The group of people in this picture are a Jewish family called the Rothschilds. They have gathered to pray. Although it is a solemn occasion, the boy on the right seems unaware of its seriousness. Look at the shadows. Can you work out where the light is coming from? [The Rothschild Family at Prayer, Moritz Daniel Oppenheim]

Find the focal point

Finding the focal point of a picture (see page 25) will help you appreciate how the artist has composed it.

What you need
- the pictures in this book
- tracing paper
- ruler
- pencil

What you do
1 Find some pictures that you like.
2 Find what you think is the focal point in each one.
3 Put a piece of tracing paper over each picture and, using a ruler and a pencil, draw lines joining up the most important things or figures. Then draw lines along any obvious straight edges in the pictures. See how many triangles and other geometric shapes you can find.

Picture a group

This method of producing a family portrait means you can paint one person at a time and then arrange the figures in an interesting composition.

What you need
- members of your family, one at a time
- easel or drawing board
- paper
- pastels or paints

What you do
1 Ask each person to pose for you separately.
2 Paint each person in a different pose. One can stand, another sit, one look straight ahead, another to the side, and so on. Keep all the portraits in proportion to each other.
3 Cut out each portrait with a pair of scissors.

4 Group them together on a piece of card. Experiment with the composition until you feel that it is balanced.
5 Glue your figures on to the card and hang your family portrait on the wall.

 # Heroes and villains

Some heroes and villains in art are real characters from history, others are imaginary or from stories. But, as far as an artist is concerned, it hardly matters. The image of a strong, courageous and honest hero or heroine conquering a weak and deceitful villain or monster makes an exciting picture.

Mythical heroes

Greek sculptors carved figures of their gods and heroes and placed them in public places. This was so that people could worship them, admire them and try to be like them.

Italian artists of the fourteenth and fifteenth centuries, such as Piero di Cosimo and Botticelli, looked

▲ *The hero in this picture is Saint George. He is killing the dragon that has captured the woman on the left. The artist has made dragon-slaying look rather easy, but other painters have interpreted the scene differently. See if you can find some examples.* [Saint George and the Dragon, *Paolo Uccello*]

28

Conventions of good and evil

When representing good and evil in pictures, artists usually follow certain conventions to make it quite clear who is the hero or heroine and who is the villain.

Good people tend to be shown wearing white clothes, evil people black clothes. Conventionally, Sir Galahad and Sir Lancelot from the legend of King Arthur, are dressed in gleaming armour riding white horses. Their enemies are invariably shown in black armour and riding black horses.

Heroes are also physically strong, good-looking and usually painted in heroic poses, like Napoleon in the picture on page 30. Evil characters on the other hand are unpleasant, even deformed. If you see Walt Disney's film, *The Sleeping Beauty*, compare the good-looking prince with the step-mother who turns into a foul witch and gives Sleeping Beauty the poisoned apple. Or compare Sigourney Weaver, the heroine in *Alien*, with the evil-looking creature she has to kill to save her friends.

Another convention is that heroes and heroines must behave honestly, whereas villains are deceitful and selfish. Comic-strip heroes, such as Flash Gordon and Batman, think only of doing good for others whereas their enemies seek power for themselves, no matter what the cost.

back to the Greek myths for inspiration. In his painting *The Birth of Venus*, Botticelli shows the goddess being born out of the foam of the sea. (Venus is the Roman name for the Greek goddess Aphrodite and *aphros* means foam in Greek.)

St George, patron saint of England, is a famous hero who killed a dragon. Paolo Uccello painted a picture of St George on a huge white horse killing a tame-looking dragon (see page 28). It is hard not to feel sorry for the dragon, which looks more like a pet than a fierce monster. See if you can find other pictures of the legend in which the dragon really does look fierce.

King Arthur and the Knights of the Round Table were heroes of the Middle Ages. Centuries later a group of English artists, called the Pre-Raphaelites, were inspired by Arthurian legends, which told of a glorious, lost age. The Pre-Raphaelites painted pictures of the Knights and their brave deeds.

Revolutionary heroes

Artists became interested in painting *real* heroes and heroines during the French Revolution, 200 years ago.

It was a very violent time. Many people died fighting on the streets. Members of the old ruling class were beheaded on the guillotine. After the revolution, ordinary people, led by Napoleon Bonaparte, set up what they hoped would be a fairer society for everyone.

French artists, such as Jacques Louis David, Eugène Delacroix and Antoine-Jean Gros, who witnessed these dramatic events, painted

◀ Napoleon Bonaparte, the hero of this picture, was a French emperor who led his army to many victories. The artist has painted him with his troops on the way to battle. He is shown as fearless, strong and handsome: a man in control of himself and his country. [Bonaparte Crossing the Alps, *Jacques Louis David*]

▼ The hero in this painting has died fighting bravely for his country. The artist has portrayed this tragic event as a quiet moment amidst the noise and chaos of war. [The Death of Major Pierson, *John Singleton Copley*]

large-scale pictures of Napoleon (see above) and other revolutionary heroes in poses that glorified them and their deeds.

Evil and beautiful

Villains are usually male, but there are some female villains in history who are often portrayed as beautiful and bewitching rather than old, wizened and nasty.

▶ *It is hard to imagine but Salome, the beautiful woman on the left of this picture, is a villain. She is dancing for King Herod who has promised to give her anything she wants in payment. He does not know that she will ask for the head of John the Baptist on a plate. This scene is packed with detail. Look at the elaborate costumes and the architecture. Which country is it set in, do you think?*
[Salome, *Gustave Moreau*]

Salome, a character from the New Testament of the Bible, is a good example. She danced for King Herod who was so taken with her that he promised her anything she wanted. She asked for the head of the prophet John the Baptist on a plate, and he had to honour his promise. The Italian artist Caravaggio showed Salome carrying the head in a basket. Aubrey Beardsley, an English artist, drew her as a menacing vamp. French painter Gustave Moreau painted her in fine clothes in a sumptuous setting.

Masks

When you wear a mask, you can pretend to be someone else. That's why masks are often used in plays or religious ceremonies. Sometimes they represent demons and monsters, sometimes princes and gods.

Most countries have a tradition of mask-making, and the variety of techniques and materials craftsmen use is enormous.

African masks are used in religious ceremonies. They are made of stone, metal, wood, ivory, the horns and teeth of animals, feathers and shells. Many of these masks represent frightening demons.

Indian masks are mostly used in dance and drama. They can be made of clay, paper or wood. They represent Indian gods and heroes from Hindu legend, such as the black goddess Kali, the five-headed creator Brahma, and the elephant-headed god, Ganesha.

The Indonesian dance drama *Calonarang* features the evil Rangda who turns in anger into the terrifying Barong. The masks used are spectacular and frightening (see below), but the story is very popular.

The best-known Japanese masks are those used in Noh theatre, plays based on Japanese myths and legends. One actor plays many different parts, and each time he changes character he changes his mask.

▼ *This picture shows a scene from the Indonesian drama* Calonarang. *The features of the mask have been exaggerated to make it look angry and evil. Notice how its eyes bulge and how long its teeth are.*

Make a list of heroes, heroines and villains from films or television programmes you have seen. Can you tell whether they are good or bad? How? By their facial expressions? The clothes they wear? The way people treat them? The music that plays every time they appear?

Make a mask

Actors in ancient Greece often wore masks with upturned or downturned mouths to show what type of play they were putting on – a comedy or a tragedy. The happy and sad masks below are modern versions. They are not worn by actors but are used as symbols to represent the theatre.

Get together with some friends and write a play about your heroes and their enemies. Then design masks to wear in the play. You could base your play on a story from a comic and use characters such as Batman and The Joker or make up entirely new characters.

What you need
- pieces of cardboard   • pencil   • scissors   • length of elastic or string   • paints

What you do
1 Draw the face you want in pencil on a piece of cardboard, keeping the outline simple. Add ears or horns or pointed ears.
2 Cut out the mask.
3 Cut holes for the eyes and mouth and nose.
4 Make two small holes on either side of the mask. This is where you will attach the string or elastic.
5 Now paint your mask.
6 Knot elastic through the holes in the sides of the mask, making it tight enough to keep the mask on your head.

6 People at work

Most people have to work. If they are not doing paid work in offices or factories or on farms, then they are running a house or looking after their children. In times of high unemployment, when there is not enough paid work for all the people who need jobs, life is often very hard.

The world of work is a rich subject for artists. Some choose to glorify work and make it look exciting; others paint more realistic pictures of the daily working life.

On the land

It is only in the last 200 years or so that people have worked in offices and factories. Before that, most people did agricultural work. They ploughed the soil, sowed and harvested crops, milked cows, and tended sheep, much like farmers do today – except that there were no machines and they did it all by hand.

The first paintings of people working in the fields are tiny illustrations that appear in the margins of

▼ *This picture shows people at work in a market in India. The man in the centre is making sweets to be sold on the stall to the left. The woman in the blue sari is selling fish. This is a very colourful scene. The artist obviously enjoyed painting all the sweets and the richly coloured clothes. Is there a market near where you live? Why not paint a picture of it?*
[Fish Seller, Sweetmeat Maker and Seller with their Wares, *Shiva Dayal Lal*]

▲ *Gustave Courbet,*
who painted this
picture, felt it was
important to record the
hard work of everyday
life. The women here are
sieving wheat to
separate the grains from
the chaff. It looks
exhausting work – the
woman on the left is
slumped with tiredness.
The painting is unusual
because the main figure
has her back to us.
[The Winnowers,
Gustave Courbet]

illuminated manuscripts,
books written and illustrated
by hand by monks during the
Middle Ages. But pictures of
working people did not
become common until the
sixteenth century, when Pieter
Brueghel started painting in
the Netherlands.

Brueghel was a great
landscape painter, but he also
painted amusing pictures of
village life. His paintings
show country people

working, eating, drinking,
fighting and playing.
Brueghel had a great affection
for village people, but he also
saw them as figures of fun.
Before him, people thought
that art should inspire noble
thoughts – paintings were
nearly always about religious
subjects – but Brueghel's aim
was to entertain. He ignored
the hard work, long hours and
poverty that were the real
story of a peasant's life.

Realism

One of the first artists to give dignity to working people in paintings was a nineteenth-century Fenchman called Gustave Courbet.

Courbet started a movement called Realism. He and a small group of artists painted truthful accounts of country life, with its hard work, poverty and suffering. Courbet felt that people who worked the land deserved as much admiration as the heroic leaders painted by David.

When Courbet first showed his pictures, people were outraged. 'These are common people,' they cried. 'What is the message? Where are the gods and angels?' Courbet replied, 'I cannot paint an angel because I have not seen one.'

Many artists followed Courbet's lead and paintings of working people became appreciated. There are no stories in these scenes, no drama or excitement. They are simple records of hard work.

Shiny new factories

In the nineteenth century, the working lives of many people changed. Fewer farm workers were needed so people moved to the towns to work in the new factories, to go down the mines, to build ships and to make cloth in the cotton mills.

This was an exciting new age and artists were keen to paint it. Fernand Léger, a French artist, was impressed with the beauty of the new machines. He was sure that they would change things for the better. His colourful pictures ignore the dirt and

▲ *This picture was painted when steel had just become a popular building material. New exciting structures were built everywhere. Léger, who painted this, was thrilled by thoughts of a new age of shiny factories and machines. Do you think his excitement comes across in the picture?* [Les Constructeurs, *Fernand Léger*]

▶ *The men in this picture are not working to make money but as a punishment. They are are prisoners on a chain gang. What kind of work are they doing? Look at the colours of their tools. Are they realistic?*
[Chain Gang, *William H. Johnson*]

grime of industry and show cheerful people working with shiny new machinery. Unlike Courbet's realistic pictures, Léger's paintings promise a bright future full of opportunities for the working man and woman.

The Futurists

A group of Italian artists, called the Futurists, went further than Léger. Their leader, the poet Filippo Marinetti, was so obsessed by the new industrial age that he completely rejected the art of the past. He even wanted museums to be destroyed. Some Futurist pictures have no figures in them at all, just huge pieces of machinery pounding away.

However, it soon became clear that the new factories were not a blessing for everyone. Small children were working long hours for very little money and people were killed by faulty machinery. The new cities became smoky, cramped and dirty. Artists such as Honoré Daumier in the nineteenth century, and the modern artist L.S. Lowry, showed the hard reality of life in the industrial age.

Domestic work

Before the invention of washing machines, vacuum cleaners and refrigerators, keeping a house was much harder work. All the chores had to be done by hand. Rich people had servants to wash, clean, cook, and lay the fires (there was no central heating). Poor people had to work for the rich and look after themselves, too. Some women took in washing to do at home. Imagine having to cart buckets of water home from a pump in the street every day, wash dozens of heavy sheets by hand, then wring them out, dry them and iron them.

The French artist Edgar Degas painted many pictures of women doing this kind of work. They look tired out and bored with the drudgery of their daily lives.

Degas painted one or two pictures of people working in offices, but there are very few pictures of this subject. Why do you think that is? Look at some books and find pictures of people working in different jobs. What kinds of work do artists like to paint?

◀ This painting shows what life was like for many women a hundred years ago, before the electric iron and the washing machine were invented. Irons had to be heated on fires and washing was all done by hand. We can tell how hard the work was by the way the women are standing. Paintings like this give us a glimpse of the lives of people from different times and places.
[The Laundresses, Edgar Degas]

The shapes of pictures

Have you ever wondered why it is that most paintings have straight edges, rather than curved ones? It is because a picture is easier to understand, or 'read', if it is a simple shape. A rectangular or square frame is window-shaped. Looking at a picture is like peeping through a window into a different world.

Most paintings that have four sides come in two basic shapes, or formats. Many of the pictures in this book are taller than they are wide. This format is called portrait. A portrait format suits paintings of standing figures and tall subjects.

A picture that is wider than it is tall has what is called a landscape format. This shape suits paintings of wide open spaces, such as the countryside and the sea.

Look at the pictures in this book and work out the format of each one.

The uniform for the job

All kinds of people have to wear uniforms to work – firefighters, nurses, police officers, car mechanics, air stewards, bus conductors, prisoners. Here's a chance to design a uniform for a job of your choice or, if you wear a uniform to school, something you would like to wear yourself.

Design hints
- Uniforms have to be practical as well as attractive. A car mechanic, for example, needs an overall with plenty of pockets for tools.
- Think about colour. Some uniforms need to stand out clearly from their surroundings – the fluorescent colours of school-crossing patrollers are an example.
- Style is important, too. Most uniforms are formal rather than casual, and they have to suit all shapes, and often be adapted for both men and women.

What you need
- sketchpad
- large sheet of paper
- pencil and rubber
- pastels or paints

What you do
1 Design a motif – a symbol of the job for which your uniform is intended. This could be a distinctive badge, or a belt buckle, or a cap, or all three. Sketch it on a separate piece of paper until you are happy with it.

2 Now design the uniform. Put in pockets, buttons, cuffs, a collar – all the details that make it special.
3 Sketch your figure, wearing the basic uniform.
4 Now fill in the distinctive details and motif.

7 People at play

When you are not working and being serious, you expect to enjoy yourself and have fun. Pictures of people playing games, eating meals together, dancing or taking part in sports often have a happy, light-hearted atmosphere.

Celebration time

Although people did not watch television or play video games in the past, many of their spare-time activities were very like our own.

Special occasions, such as birthday parties or weddings, have always brought large numbers of people together. There is an air of excitement as, dressed in their best clothes, people meet up and talk over a good meal.

Pieter Brueghel, who painted the working life of

▼ *Although this picture of a wedding is over 400 years old, it looks familiar. The clothes are different from today's but the event is the same. Can you see the bride? She is sitting in front of the black curtain. The artist has included many people in the picture, yet it does not look crowded. How do you think he managed this? [Peasant Wedding, Pieter Brueghel]*

Chorus line

Dancers were a favourite subject of the artist Edgar Degas. Make this chain silhouette of dancers and try to capture the lively movements of a chorus line.

What you need
- long strip of paper, not too thick
- pencil
- scissors
- pastels or paints

What you do
1 Fold the paper in a concertina shape.
2 Draw a dancer on the front end of the concertina shape. Make your figure full of movement, but also make sure its hands and legs touch each side of the paper.

3 Cut round the shape through all the thicknesses of paper at once.
4 Unfold the paper to reveal a line of dancers.
5 Using pastels or paints, give each dancer different features, hairstyle and clothes.

villagers so well, also painted wonderful party pictures (see facing page). Although he lived over 400 years ago, his party-goers eat, listen to music, play games and chatter just like people today. Brueghel liked to include many activities in one picture. Look in the corners of his pictures, and around the edges; you will usually find something amusing.

Another Dutch artist, Jan Steen, who lived a hundred years after Brueghel, was the landlord of an inn. He liked to include his own customers in his pictures of people enjoying themselves.

Turn to the sports pages of a newspaper and look for some dramatic photographs. Sports photographers have to think and act quickly and may have to take several rolls of film before getting the right shot. Good sports pictures show people stretching their bodies to the limit and can be full of emotion – the joy of winning, the despair of losing, the pain of an injury. Find a really thrilling picture of your favourite sports person. How do you think he or she is feeling? Why?

◄ *In nineteenth-century Paris, many dances were held outside. They were lively occasions and full of fun. Auguste Renoir, who painted this picture of one such dance, has captured the excitement and pleasure. By using many small brush-strokes, he has created a feeling of movement and gaiety.*
[Dance at the Bougival, *Auguste Renoir*]

The great outdoors

Although landscapes – pictures of the countryside – have been popular for 300 years, few artists actually painted out of doors until the nineteenth century. The eighteenth-century Frenchman, Watteau, was an exception, but he did not paint real people in real settings. He dreamt up magical places where beautiful people in fine clothes amused themselves.

It was a group of French painters, called the Impressionists, who started the trend for taking easel and paints outside. This was called painting *en plein air* (see below). The Impressionists painted things very quickly because they wanted to capture movement in their pictures. As a result, their paintings are made up of lots of short, dashing brushstrokes that flicker across the canvas.

The Impressionist Auguste Renoir visited cafés, open-air dance halls, parks and boating parties to find good subjects. His pictures are cheerful and full of sunshine and happiness.

Renoir used summery colours in these pictures and applied the paint with soft, feathery brushstrokes. This technique suited his subjects very well: the figures in his pictures dance and laugh in the dappled sunshine.

The Impressionists *en plein air*

The French phrase for 'out of doors' is *en plein air*. One of the leading Impressionists, Claude Monet, urged his friends to abandon their studios altogether. He had a little boat fitted out as a studio so that he could paint the river from close quarters whenever he wanted.

Monet and other Impressionists found that painting outside required a different technique from painting indoors. Clouds, bustling crowds and rippling water all move so quickly that there was no time to mix colours on the palette. Instead they dabbed the colours straight on to the canvas from the tubes. Often they put the paint on with a knife rather than a brush.

The Impressionists avoided dark, earthy colours, preferring primary colours – red, yellow and blue. All other colours can be mixed from combinations of these three. You might think this technique would limit the colours of their paintings. But it did not. If you look at an Impressionist picture, you think you see more colours than there are. The dabs of colour are so close together that they seem to merge into all kinds of different colours as you look at them. The colours printed on the pages of this book are also made of dots. Look at one of the pictures through a magnifying glass and you will see how your naked eye is deceived.

Indoor games

Do you ever play board games or cards at home? Think how people sit when they are concentrating on their next move. They are often quiet, occasionally noisy, sometimes serious. They frown a bit, sigh, smile secretly, put their heads in their hands, get excited when they win.

Pictures of indoor games may lack the gaiety of outdoor scenes but they show people's thoughts and feelings more clearly. For example, Paul Cézanne, a French artist, painted a picture of three men sitting round a table playing cards and enjoying each other's company. Another Frenchman, Jean Baptiste Siméon Chardin, painted pictures of solitary children absorbed in card games. The American artist Horace Pippin painted a family playing dominoes in the 1940s (see above). Look at the people's faces. What are the players thinking?

The sporting life

The first Olympic Games were held in ancient Greece 2,500 years ago. Statues of famous athletes were displayed outside temples for people to admire. Sporting events of all kinds – and images of them – have been with us ever since.

▲ *Look closely at this picture and see how much you can learn about the people in it. Who is winning the game and who is losing? Are the people rich or poor? What is the seated woman making? What time of day is it? The more you look at a painting the more you can discover about it.*
[Domino Players, Horace Pippin]

Create a masterpiece

Copying a famous painting teaches you a great deal about the artist's technique. This picture, a copy of Auguste Renoir's *Dance at the Bougival* (see page 42), was painted by a young person.

What you need

- a famous picture that you like, from this book or another
- large piece of paper
- pencil for sketching
- paints – if possible, try to use the same kind of paints as the artist you are copying

What you do

1 Look at your picture carefully, noting the colours the artist has used and how the picture is composed. This means the size and position of each object or figure in the picture.
2 Look at the brushstrokes. Are they big and sweeping or small and smooth?
3 Mix up a palette of colours, matching those in the picture as closely as possible.
4 Sketch the outlines in pencil. Take care over this.

5 Now start to paint. Don't worry if your picture isn't exactly the same as the one you are copying. Even the world's most successful forgers take years to learn how to copy a painting exactly.

▼ *This archery contest is taking place in ancient China. The men wearing blue are the judges. Notice how the figure on the horse has been painted smaller to create a feeling of depth. The picture was painted on silk. What effect do you think this has on the way the painting looks?*

Quiet sports, such as archery and golf, are easier to paint than fast-moving ones. With those, the artist may have no chance to make an accurate record of events. He or she has to capture the impression of the event with fast brushstrokes or sketches that can be worked up later. Some artists take photographs instead and use them as the basis for a picture.

About the artists

BRUEGHEL, Pieter the Elder (c. 1525-1569) Brueghel was an artist from the Netherlands who painted in a style unlike that of anyone else at the time. He painted the countryside and the people who worked the land.

CASSATT, Mary (1845-1926) Although Mary Cassatt was born in America she spent much of her time in Paris, France. She liked to paint pictures of everyday life.

COPLEY, John Singleton (1737-1815) This American painter spent most of his life in Italy and France. He specialized in painting portraits and large historical paintings.

COURBET, Gustave (1819-1877) When this French painter first exhibited his pictures of the everyday life of the poor, there was a huge outcry. This new way of painting, Realism, had not been seen before in art.

DAVID, Jacques Louis (1748-1825) The most important painter in France during the French Revolution. He painted pictures of heroes and victories of the revolution.

DEGAS, Edgar (1834-1917) This French painter was one of the first artists to paint the world around him. His subjects include dancers, the races, town life, places of work, places of entertainment and portraits.

DURER, Albrecht (1471-1528) A German artist who became well known for his woodcuts of Biblical stories. He was an expert engraver and painter, recording the world around him with great skill and accuracy.

GAINSBOROUGH, Thomas (1727-1788) Gainsborough was the leading portrait painter in England during the eighteenth century. He painted many members of the aristocracy and wealthy landowners.

HALS, Frans (c. 1580-1666) This Dutch painter was a popular portrait painter in the town of Haarlem where he lived. He painted portraits of people on their own and in large groups.

HOLBEIN, Hans (1497-1543) Holbein began painting portraits of wealthy businessmen in Germany. He later moved to England where he became court painter to Henry VIII.

JOHNSON, William Henry (1843-1942) Best known as a photographer, Johnson took pictures of landscapes, especially the dramatic scenery of the American West.

LEGER, Fernand (1881-1955) Léger was a French painter who began his career as a Cubist. Later, he tried to capture the beauty of machinery and the strength of the working man with bright colours and black outlines.

LEONARDO DA VINCI (1452-1519) Leonardo was not only a painter and sculptor but also an architect, inventor, scientist, writer and musician. He left very few paintings but these, along with numerous drawings and sketches, have been very influential. He used thin glazes to create an effect called *sfumato*.

MICHELANGELO Buonarroti (1475-1564) An Italian painter and sculptor who was highly regarded during his lifetime and hugely influential after it. His most famous painting, on the Sistine Chapel ceiling in Rome, took him over four years to finish.

MOORE, Henry ((1898-1986) Although this English artist sculpted figures, he was not interested in the details. Instead he created figures that were based on the human body and inspired by other natural shapes.

MOREAU, Gustave (1826-1898) This French artist favoured large, biblical or classical subjects, which he painted in great detail.

OPPENHEIM, Moritz Daniel (1800-1882) An American artist known for his paintings of groups of people.

PIPPIN, Horace (1888-1946) One of the first black artists to be widely appreciated in North America. *The Domino Players* (on page 44) is one of his best-known pictures.

REMBRANDT, Harmensz van Rijn (1606-1669) Although this Dutch artist left 600 oil paintings, 1,500 drawings and 350 etchings, he died a pauper. He was a master of capturing the effects of light, the emotions of his subjects and the textures of fabric.

RENOIR, Auguste (1841-1919) This French artist's work is full of sunshine and gaiety. He was especially good at painting the dappled shadows of summer and life outdoors.

ROCKWELL, Norman (1894-1978) Most of the work of this American painter and illustrator appeared in the newspaper the *Saturday Evening Post*. His pictures are very detailed and accurate, and often humorous.

STRANG, William (1859-1921) Born in Scotland, Strang later moved to London where he painted many portraits of 'smart' society. He used striking compositions and bold colours.

UCCELLO, Paolo (c. 1396-1475) A painter from Florence, Italy, who was fascinated with the problems of how to show three dimensions (solid shapes) on a two-dimensional (flat) surface. He was one of the first artists to develop linear perspective.

VAN GOGH, Vincent (1853-1890) Today, Van Gogh's paintings sell for millions of pounds, but during his lifetime he sold only one picture. He suffered from fits of madness and depression, and his paintings, with their intense colours and frenzied brushstrokes, reflect his disturbed life.

WOOD, Grant (1891-1942) An American artist who painted scenes of the landscape and community there. He is best known for his painting called *American Gothic*, which appears on page 14.

Acknowledgements

ZEFA/Sharp Shooters, p.18 (bottom); by kind permission of the Henry Moore Foundation, p.20; Werner Forman Archive, p.32; The Phillips Collection, Washington, USA, p.44.

All other pictures are from the Bridgeman Art Library, courtesy of the following organizations: Christie's, London, p.4; Prado, Madrid, p.6; Galleria degli Uffizi, Florence, p.7 (left); National Gallery, London, pp.7 (right), 12 (bottom), 22, 28; Courtauld Institute Galleries, University of London, p.9 and *cover*; Louvre, Paris, p.10; Thyssen-Bornemisza Collection, Madrid, p.11; Museum für Volkerkunde, Berlin, p.12 (top); Art Institute of Chicago, USA, p.14; National Archaeological Museum, Athens, p.16; Museum für Volkerkunde, Vienna, p.17; Museo dell'Opera del Duomo, Florence/Index, p.18 (top); Forbes Magazine Collection, London, p.24; private collections, pp.25, 31; Roy Miles Gallery, London, W1, p.26; Château de Malmaison, Paris/Giraudon, p.30 (top); Tate Gallery, London, p.30 (bottom); India Office Library, London, p.34; Musée des Beaux-Arts, Nantes/Giraudon, p.35; Musée Léger, Biot, © DACS 1994, p.36; National Museum of American Art, Smithsonian Inst. copyright and Permlet Art Resource, p.37; Musée d'Orsay, Paris/ Giraudon p.38; Kunsthistorisches Museum, Vienna, p.40; Museum of Fine Arts, Boston, Massachusetts, p.42; the Board of Trustees of the Victoria and Albert Museum, London, p.45.

The illustrations in this book are all by Annabel Spenceley.

If copyright in any picture reproduced in this book has unwittingly been infringed, Touchstone Publishing Ltd apologizes and will pay an appropriate fee to the rightful owner as if we had been able to obtain prior permission.

Index